NOT THE WORST THING EVER!

A Gross, Giggly Guide to Dealing with Diabetes

POKE PRIZE PRESS

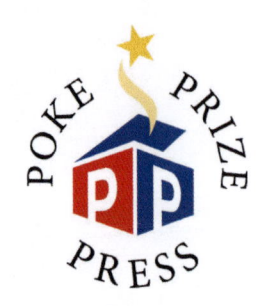

www.pokeprizepress.com

No part of this publication may be reproduced, stored in a retrieval system, or transmitted in any form or by any means, electronic, mechanical, photocopying, recording, or otherwise, without the written permission of the publisher. For information regarding permission, write to Poke Prize Press, LLC, 3230 Sycamore Rd #160, DeKalb, IL, 60115

ISBN 978-1-957266-00-8

Text and Illustrations copyright ©2022 by Poke Prize Press, LLC. All Rights Reserved.

Poke Prize Press is a publisher of fun, informative books designed to help people live well with Type 1 Diabetes.

For more information, or to enquire about special or bulk orders, contact us through our website:
www.pokeprizepress.com

Note: This book is meant to entertain kids and adults. It should not be used to make decisions about diabetes care. For more information, talk to your endocrinologist or consult manufacturer's guides and websites.

NOT THE WORST THING EVER!
A GROSS, GIGGLY GUIDE TO DEALING WITH DIABETES

Written by
Gillian King-Cargile

Illustrated by
Shawn Turek

You think getting a finger stick is the worst thing ever?

HA! NOT A CHANCE. I CAN THINK OF A HUNDRED THINGS THAT ARE A HUNDRED TIMES WORSE.

Like wearing a turtleneck shirt...

...made of diapers...

...filled with asparagus pee...

...for an entire school day.

Or taking a bath...

...in a huge, splintery barrel...

...of warm baby boogers.

AND YES, YOU HAVE TO DUNK YOUR HEAD TO WASH YOUR HAIR.

A finger stick doesn't sound so bad.

You think getting a shot is the worst thing ever?

OH PLEASE! I CAN THINK OF A THOUSAND THINGS THAT ARE A THOUSAND TIMES WORSE.

Like eating a baked bologna and Band-Aid sandwich...

...served on a whole wheat roll sprouting

mini mushy mountains of mold...

...sitting on a plate of sweaty socks and sauerkraut.

And you have to wash the meal down with
a glass of hot, chunky whole milk.

Or walking a pirate's plank...

...into a sea of sewage.

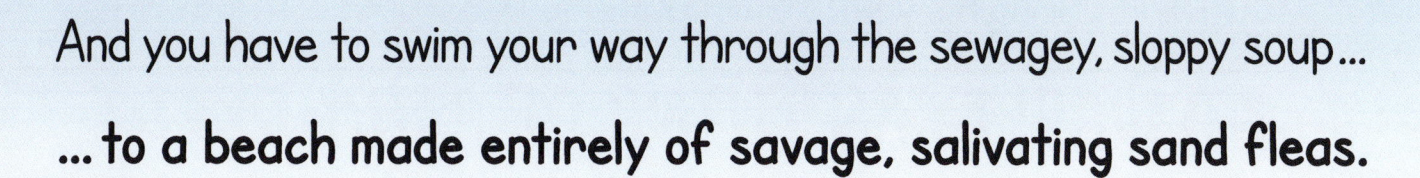

And you have to swim your way through the sewagey, sloppy soup...

... to a beach made entirely of savage, salivating sand fleas.

Getting a shot doesn't sound so bad.

You think changing your insulin pump is the worst thing ever?

NO WAY! I CAN THINK OF A HUNDRED THOUSAND THINGS THAT ARE A HUNDRED THOUSAND TIMES WORSE.

MENU

APPETIZER

MAIN COURSE

DESSERT

Like being eaten by a great white shark...

...that also ate a school of peevish puffer fish as an appetizer...

...and a tangle of angry electric eels as dessert.

And then the great white shark gets an explosive case of great green diarrhea.

Or having a clown-themed birthday party.

Like *extremely* clown-themed.

That's all. Clowns are terrifying.

What are they hiding under all that makeup?

Changing your insulin pump doesn't sound so bad.

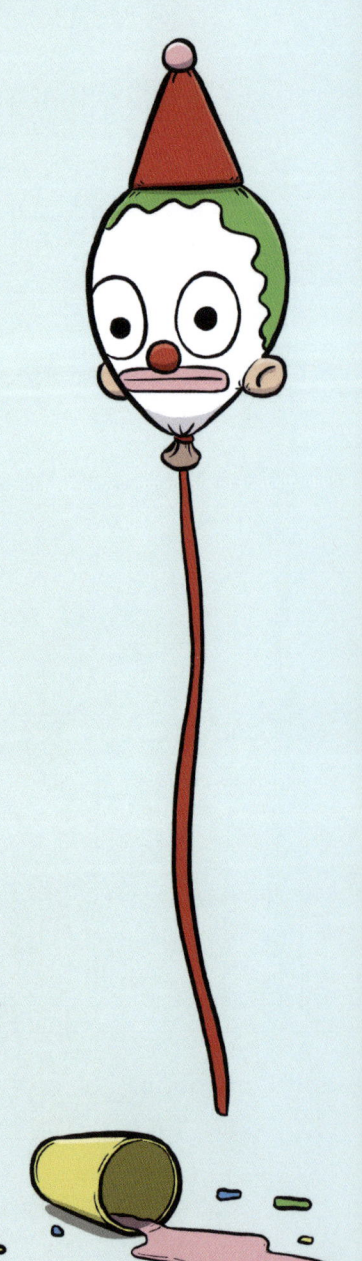

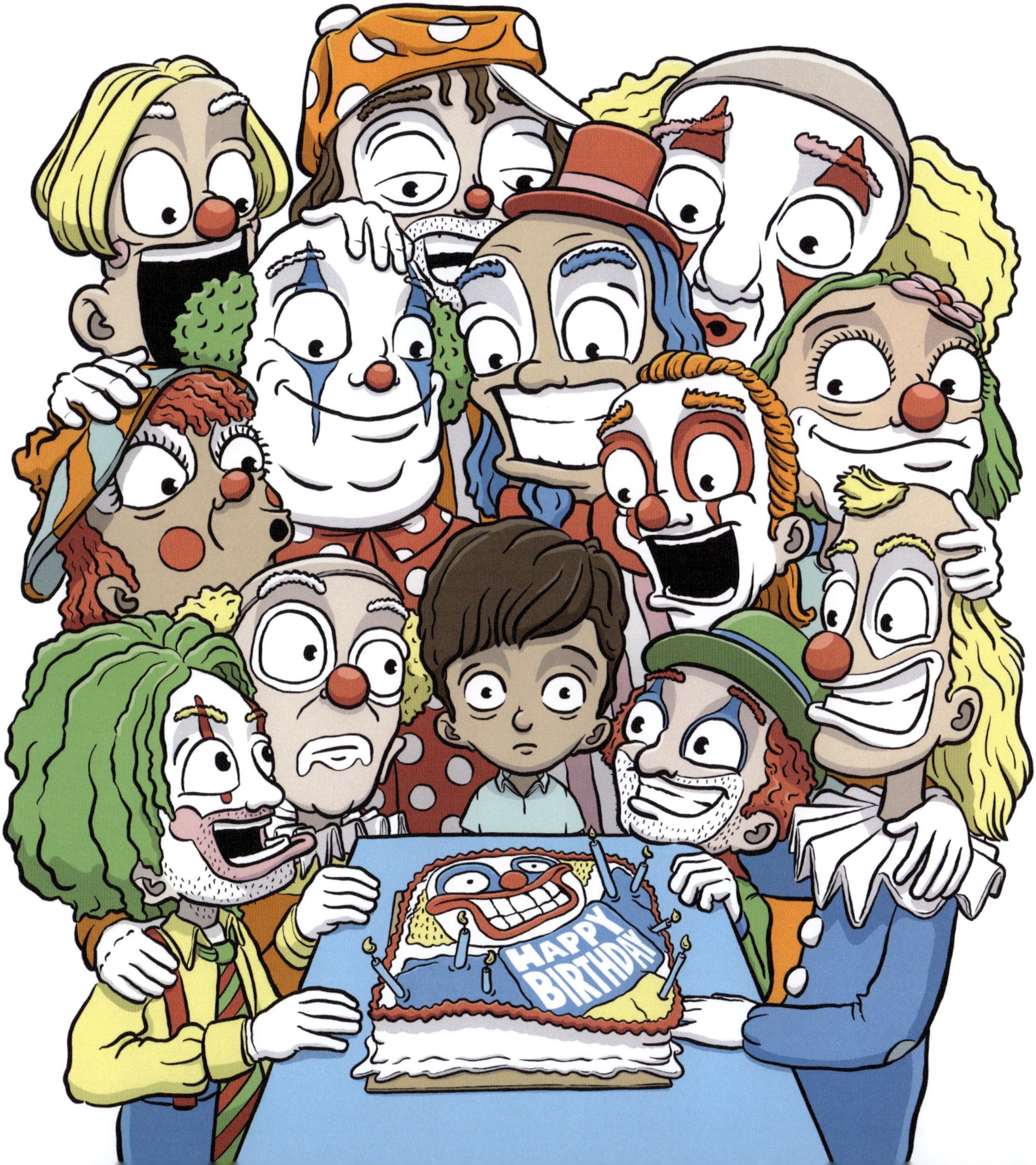
HAPPY BIRTHDAY

You think changing your continuous glucose monitor is the worst thing ever?

NOT EVEN CLOSE! I CAN THINK OF A MILLION THINGS THAT ARE A MILLION TIMES WORSE.

Like combing your hair...

...which is made of wet, wiggly earthworms...

...that smear slippery slicks of worm slime across your forehead.

But don't worry. You can wash your face clean in a bird bath full of starving robins.

Or being abducted by aliens...

...who want to flip you inside out.

FLIPMASTER INSIDE-OUT-A-TRON 8000

Just for fun!

They're not even trying to learn anything from it.

Did I mention they don't know how to flip you back?

And it's picture day at school.

Class of 2?

Changing your continuous glucose monitor doesn't sound so bad.

You know what's the best thing ever?

DOING WHAT YOU NEED TO DO TO STAY HEALTHY.

So stick out your finger.

Get the shot.

Change your pump site.

Click on that new CGM.

Or do you want me to start filling up that booger barrel?

NO?

Phew!

I was gagging just thinking about collecting all those buckets of baby snot.

Just remember:

YOU'RE BRAVE.

YOU'RE STRONG.

THIS IS NOT THE WORST THING EVER.

YOU'VE GOT THIS!

WHY IS THIS BOOK SO GROSS?!

Sometimes dealing with your Type 1 Diabetes can be a challenge. While you might want to ignore it or run away from it or even scream and cry, the best way to stay healthy is to monitor and control your blood sugar. That might mean getting a finger stick, getting a shot, changing your pump site, or changing your continuous glucose monitor.

While all those pokes and shots and jabs might not be any fun, they're a lot better than getting sick. They're also a lot better than getting gobbled up and pooped out by a shark!

NOW IT'S YOUR TURN TO GET GROSS!

If you're giggling and gagging and grossing yourself out, a poke might not seem so bad. Try to think of some weird, stinky, pukey things that would be way worse than being brave about your Type 1 Diabetes treatments.

Use the sentences below to make up your own examples.

> Getting a finger poke is a lot better than…

> Getting a shot is a lot better than…

> Changing my pump site is a lot better than…

> Changing my continuous glucose monitor is a lot better than…

Gosh! I can't believe you said those things! You're really gross.

HEALTHY, BRAVE, AND TOTALLY GROSS!

For everyone touched by Type 1.
We need all the laughs we can get!

- GKC

For my wife and daughter, who encourage
and inspire me to keep creating.

- ST

POKE PRIZE PRESS

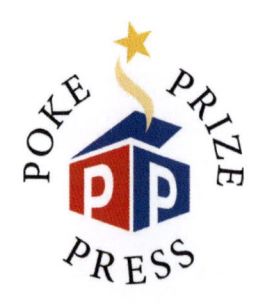

Join our email list to find more fun, informative books designed to help people live well with Type 1 Diabetes.

www.pokeprizepress.com

Also Available from Poke Prize Press:

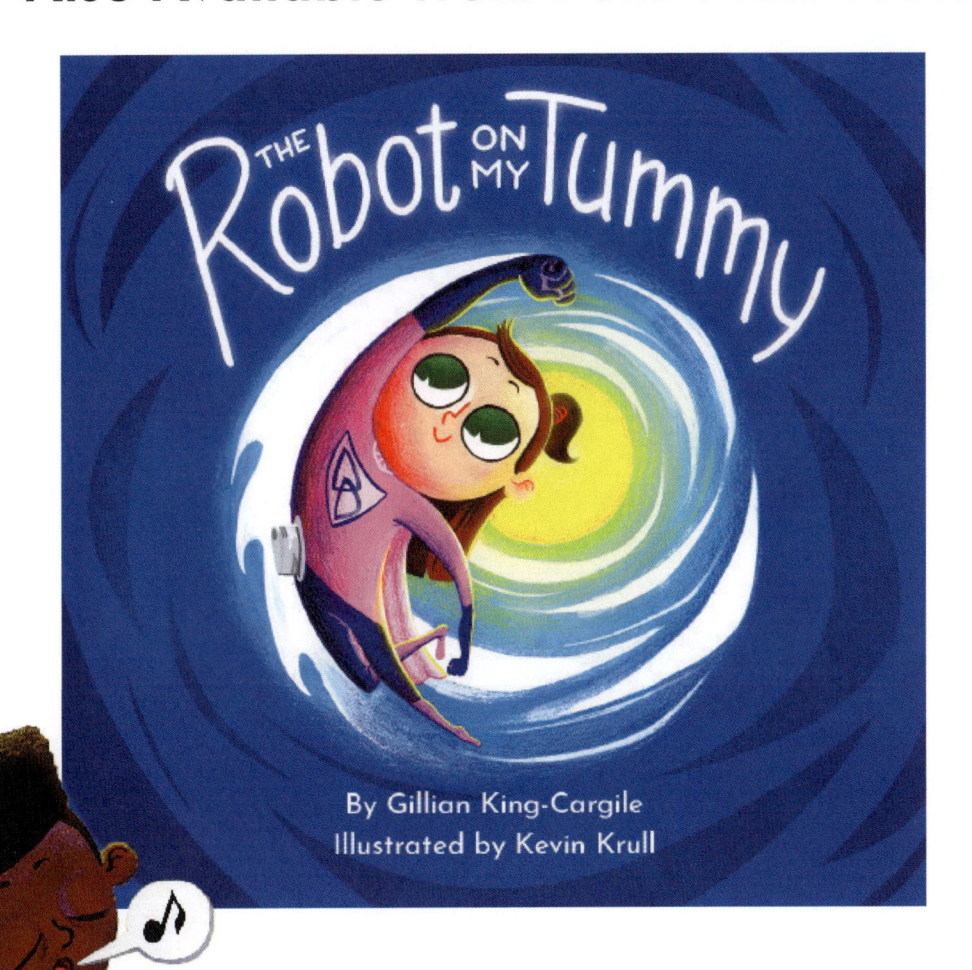

The Robot on My Tummy

By Gillian King-Cargile
Illustrated by Kevin Krull

This rhyming picture book takes T1D kids on an imaginative journey through the ways a Continuous Glucose Monitor (CGM) can change their diabetes routine for the better.

Printed in Great Britain
by Amazon